THE ART OF MODULATING
FOR PIANISTS & JAZZ

BY CARLOS SALZEDO
& LUCILE LAWRENCE

ISBN 978-1-4584-1146-4

G. Schirmer, Inc.

DISTRIBUTED BY

7777 W. BLUEMOUND RD. P.O. BOX 13819 MILWAUKEE, WI 53213

In Australia Contact:
Hal Leonard Australia Pty. Ltd.
4 Lentara Court
Cheltenham, Victoria, 3192 Australia
Email: ausadmin@halleonard.com.au

No part of this publication may be reproduced in any form or by any means
without the prior written permission of the Publisher.

Copyright © 1950, 2012 by G. Schirmer, Inc. (ASCAP) New York, NY
International Copyright Secured   All Rights Reserved

Visit Hal Leonard Online at
www.halleonard.com

FOREWORD

Carlos Salzedo's knowledge of classical and contemporary music is profound. His views on the gradual harmonic motion from one key center to another, or the sudden violent contrasts of key relations, and the synchronous sounding of distantly-related harmonies are of great value to students and to all those interested in the nature of music.

Lucile Lawrence is not only a brilliant virtuoso but an orchestra, radio, and television harpist who understands the relation of her instrument to the full orchestral design. Her great talent and experience make her an ideal co-author with Carlos Salzedo for a book on the "art of modulating."

In presenting modulation as an individual principle not merely as a by-product of harmony, this book will be a revelation to musicians in the application of music to modern practical usage.

Leopold Stokowski

INTRODUCTION

This treatise has been made as simple and concise as the subject permits. It was primarily intended exclusively for harpists but was found to be adaptable to the needs of organists and pianists. The modulating formulas given herein are by no means the only ones that can be used, but they have been selected in preference to others because they are short and harmonically correct and, therefore, practical. These formulas consist of not more than three chords: 1) the tonic triad (root position) of the key of the composition just ended; 2) a transitory chord; 3) the dominant seventh (root position) of the key of the composition that follows. In some instances only two chords are necessary: 1) the tonic triad (root position) of the key of the composition just ended; 2) the dominant seventh (root position) of the key of the composition that follows.

This book, having been prepared mainly for the use of instrumentalists with slight knowledge of harmony, does not include ninth chords, suspensions, and other elaborate harmonic devices in the formulas. As the instrumentalist acquires a feeling for modulating, he or she should abandon the exclusive use of the triad chord so as to adorn the modulation with richer harmonies. This, however, must not be attempted prematurely, because it might bring too much abruptness or awkwardness into the modulation.

One will find a few examples of modulating improvisations; but inasmuch as the art of modulating implies the art of improvising, it goes without saying that the modulating improvisations should be left to the skill and imagination of the instrumentalist.

CONTENTS

Table of Intervals. 4

Rules Governing Modulation 4

Modulation Formulas 6

Examples of Modulation. 28

Types of Arpeggios for Extension. 35

Ten Extensions of 10 Seconds Each and a Coda 36

Modulating Arpeggios and Chords. 38

Two Cadenzas. 39

Ten Fragments of Dances 40

Five Easy Characteristic Pieces for Keyboard 40

    Waltz Accompaniment 41

    Petite Valse 42

    Gavotte 44

    Menuet 45

    Polka. 46

    Siciliana. 47

    Bolero 48

    Seguidilla 49

    Tango. 50

    Rumba. 51

    Lullaby (Berceuse) 52

    Rêverie 54

    Carillon 56

    Grandmother's Spinning Wheel 58

    Florentine Music Box 60

TABLE OF INTERVALS

RULES GOVERNING MODULATION

Rule I
The laws for modulating are based upon the usage of chords definitely related through common tones or neighboring keys.

Rule II
Skill in the art of modulating consists in progressing from one key to another as rapidly and smoothly as possible, just as one motion picture scene blends into another.

Rule III
When a modulation is used to pass from one key to another, as well as to fill in time between two selections, it is highly advisable to go directly into the next key and then improvise therein as long as necessary.

Rule IV
Except in very rare cases, modulating improvisations should always begin with the tonic triad of the composition just ended.

Rule V
The dominant seventh (root position) of the new key must always be used as the final chord in all modulations. Since the dominant seventh is identical in major and minor keys of the same tonality, it is immaterial, as far as the new key is concerned, whether the progression is from major to major, major to minor, minor to major, or minor to minor. Moreover, the dominant seventh, in its root position, creates an impression of "open door," which cannot be created with any other chord (ninths are too ornate and involve major and minor considerations, thus complicating the process to no advantage). This impression of "open door" is essential to introduce a composition auspiciously. Under no circumstances should the modulation terminate on the tonic triad of the new composition; this detestable habit is like corking a bottle at the moment one is about to pour the wine, and then uncorking it! Furthermore, the dominant seventh chord in its root position is best fitted to precede any beginning, whether the new composition begins with the tonic triad or with the most dissonant chord.

Rule VI
In making up modular patterns in arpeggios and chord formations, inexperienced players are inclined to start the left hand with the tonic triad in the conventional order (in the key of C, for instance: C-E-G-C). This sounds bad. The two lowest notes (left hand) of the tonic triad (root position)—chords or arpeggios—must *always* be the *root* and the *fifth*. The only exception to this rule is when foundation chords or arpeggios are not started from the low register up, but used only in the high register.

Rule VII
The instrumentalist should modulate preferably with thematic material borrowed from the composition preceding the modulation rather than use mere chords and arpeggios, but under no circumstances should thematic material be borrowed from the next composition. The thematic material of a modulation may be reminiscent but must never divulge the composition that follows. No matter how cleverly presented, a modulation divulging the next composition would detract from its interest.

Rule VIII
During the modulation process it is of primary importance that the instrumentalist visualize the four notes which constitute the dominant seventh of the new key.

HOW TO STUDY THIS BOOK

1. Memorize the table of intervals.
2. Memorize enharmonics.
3. Be thoroughly familiar with all the major and minor keys and their respective signatures.
4. Do not merely read, but practice all modulating formulas.
5. Transpose and adapt the examples of modulation to all modulating formulas.

MODULATION FORMULAS

To modulate a minor second up from major keys:
1. Tonic triad (root position) of major key of departure
2. Tonic triad of parallel minor (root position)
3. Dominant seventh (root position) of new key

To modulate a minor second up from minor keys:
1. Tonic triad (root position) of minor key of departure
2. Dominant seventh (root position) of new key

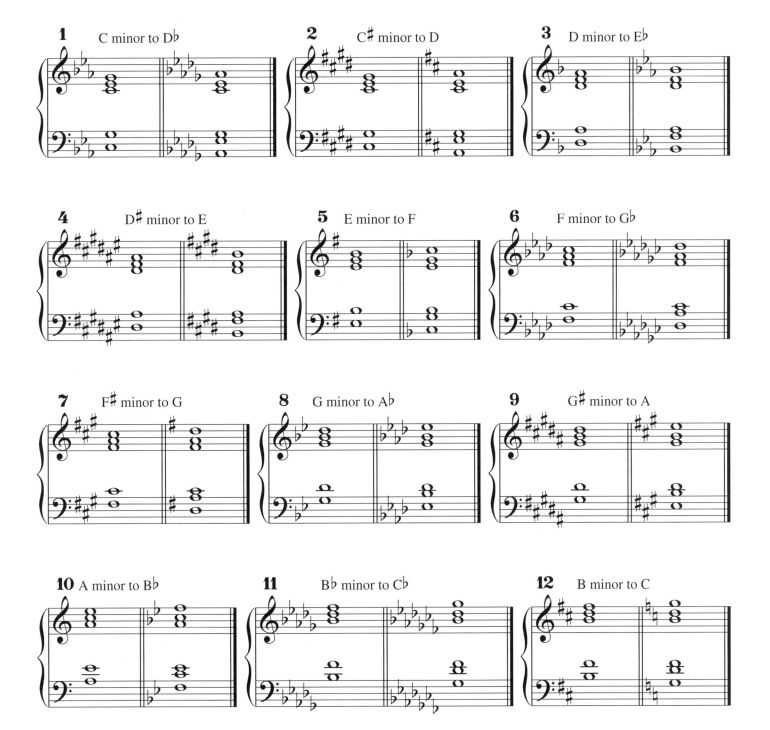

To modulate a minor second down from major keys:

1. Tonic triad (root position) of major key of departure
2. Minor triad (root position) a major third higher
3. Dominant seventh (root position) of new key

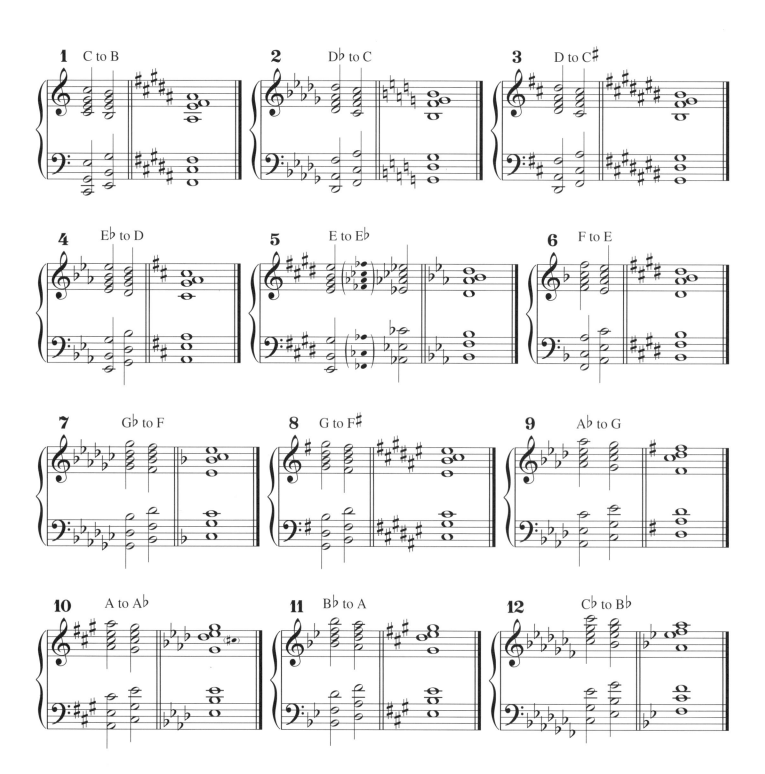

To modulate a minor second down from minor keys:
1. Tonic triad (root position) of minor key of departure
2. Minor triad (root position) a major third higher
3. Dominant seventh (root position) of new key

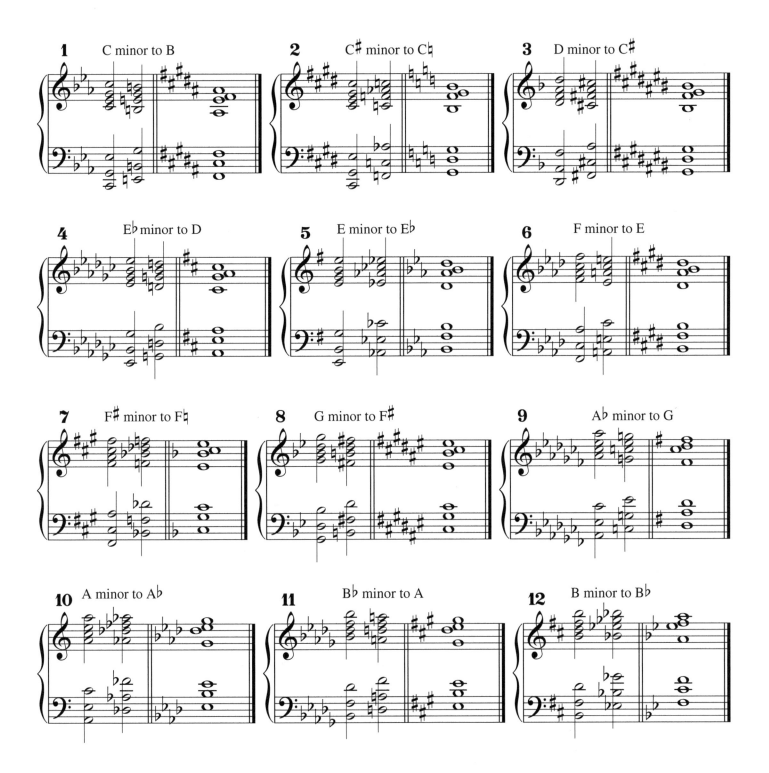

To modulate a major second up from major keys:

1. Tonic triad (root position) of major key of departure
2. Minor triad (root position) a major third higher
3. Dominant seventh (root position) of new key

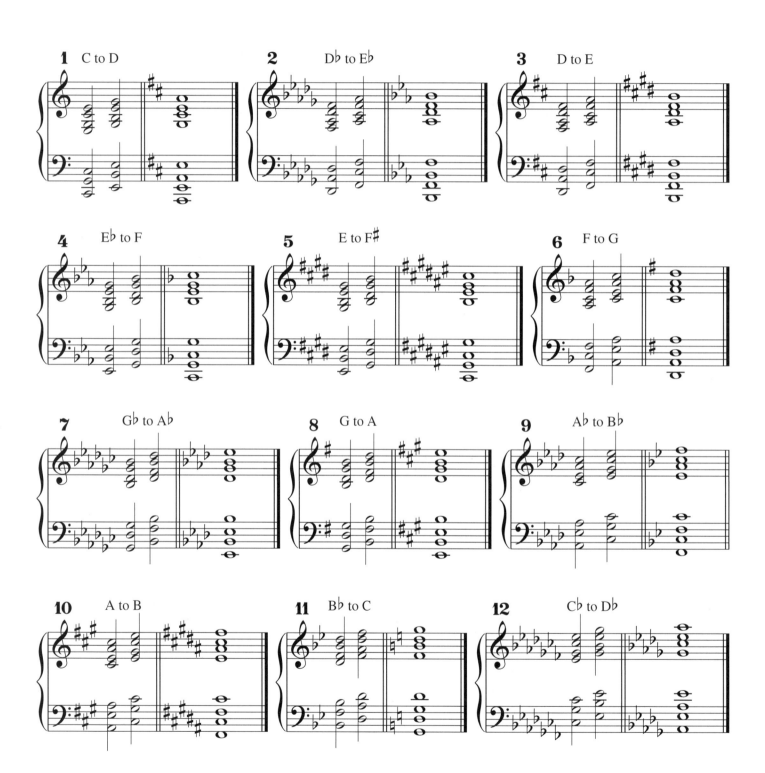

To modulate a major second up from minor keys:
1. Tonic triad (root position) of minor key of departure
2. Minor triad (root position) a major third higher
3. Dominant seventh (root position) of new key

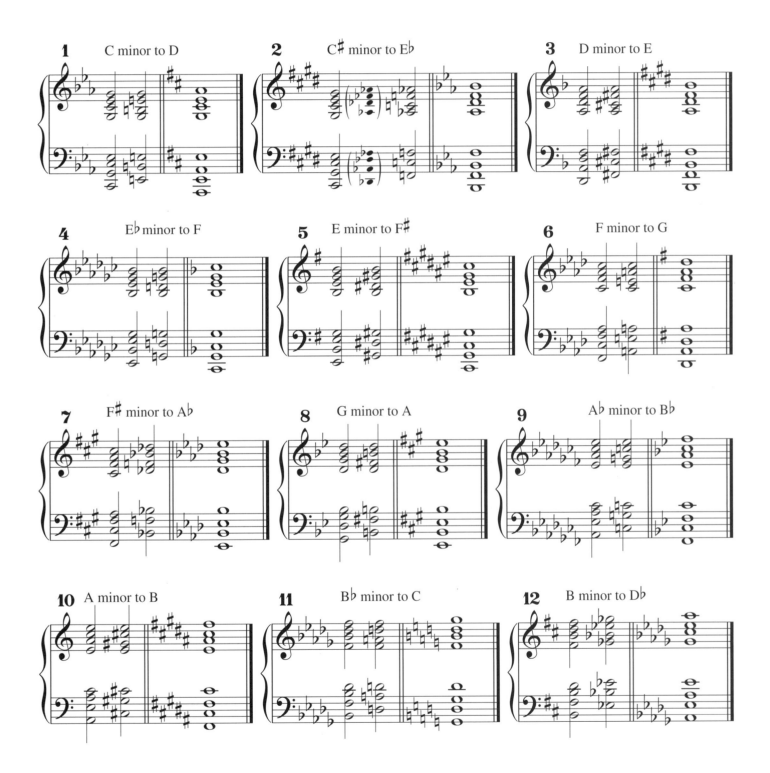

To modulate a major second down from major keys:

1. Tonic triad (root position) of major key of departure
2. Tonic triad of parallel minor (root position)
3. Dominant seventh (root position) of new key

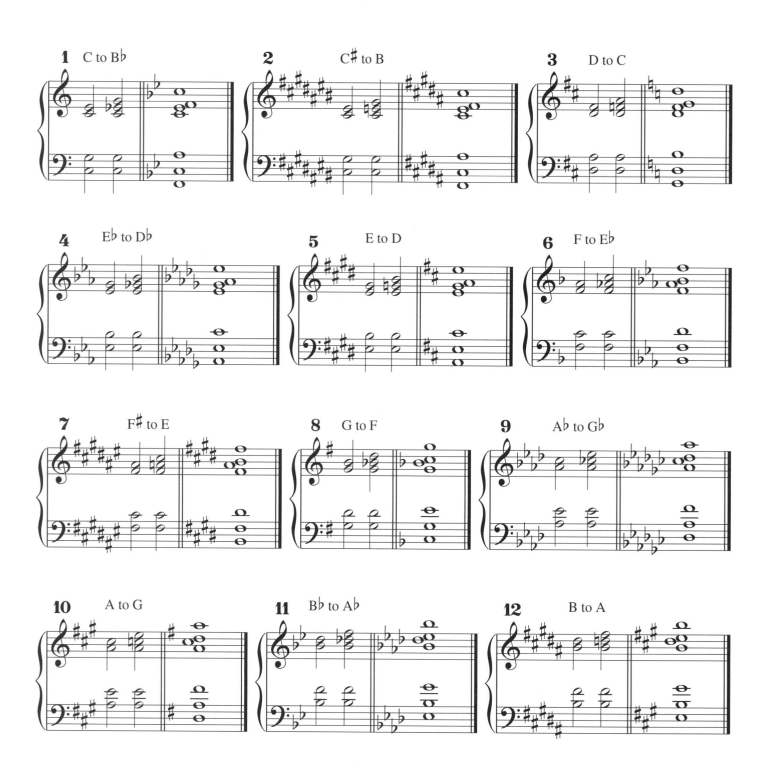

To modulate a major second down from minor keys:
1. Tonic triad (root position) of minor key of departure
2. Dominant seventh (root position) of new key

To modulate a minor third up from major keys:

1. Tonic triad (root position) of major key of departure
2. Minor triad (root position) on subdominant
3. Dominant seventh (root position) of new key

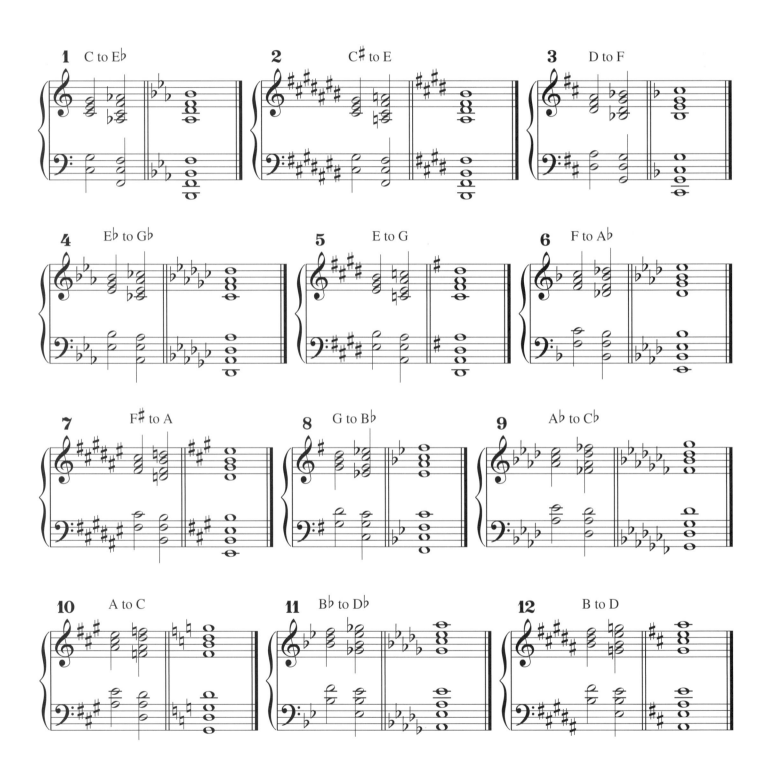

To modulate a minor third up from minor keys:
1. Tonic triad (root position) of minor key of departure
2. Minor triad (root position) on subdominant
3. Dominant seventh (root position) of new key

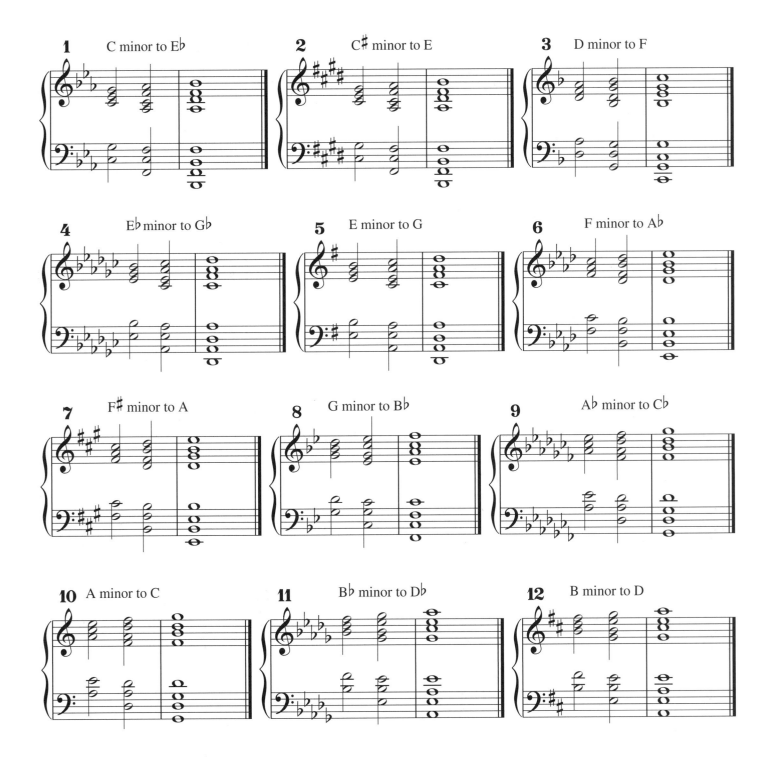

To modulate a minor third down from major keys:
1. Tonic triad (root position) of major key of departure
2. Minor triad (root position) one whole tone higher
3. Dominant seventh (root position) of new key

To modulate a minor third down from minor keys:
1. Tonic triad (root position) of minor key of departure
2. Minor triad (root position) on subdominant
3. Dominant seventh (root position) of new key

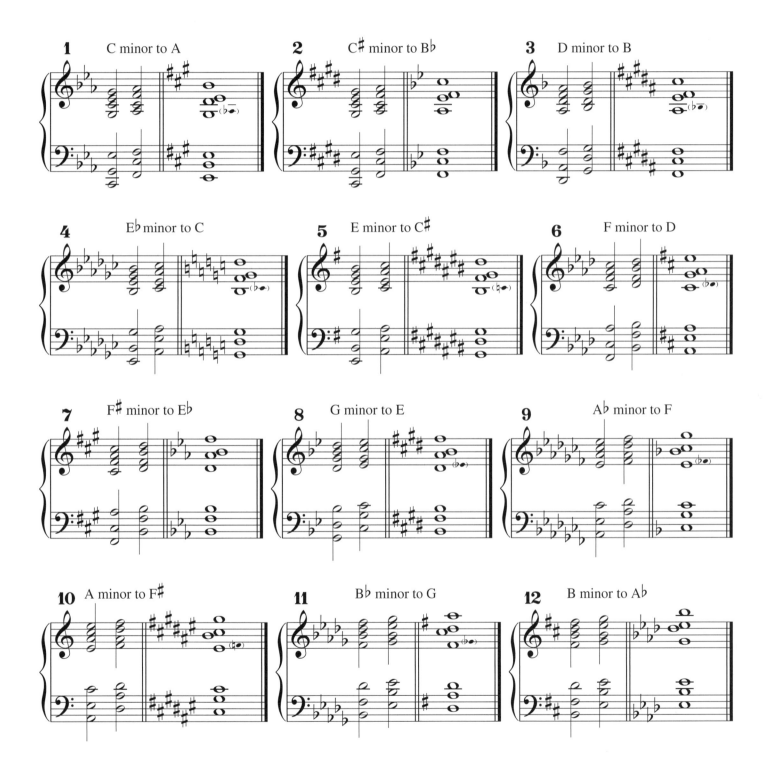

To modulate a major third up from major keys:

1. Tonic triad (root position) of major key of departure
2. Minor triad (root position) a minor third lower (relative minor)
3. Dominant seventh (root position) of new key

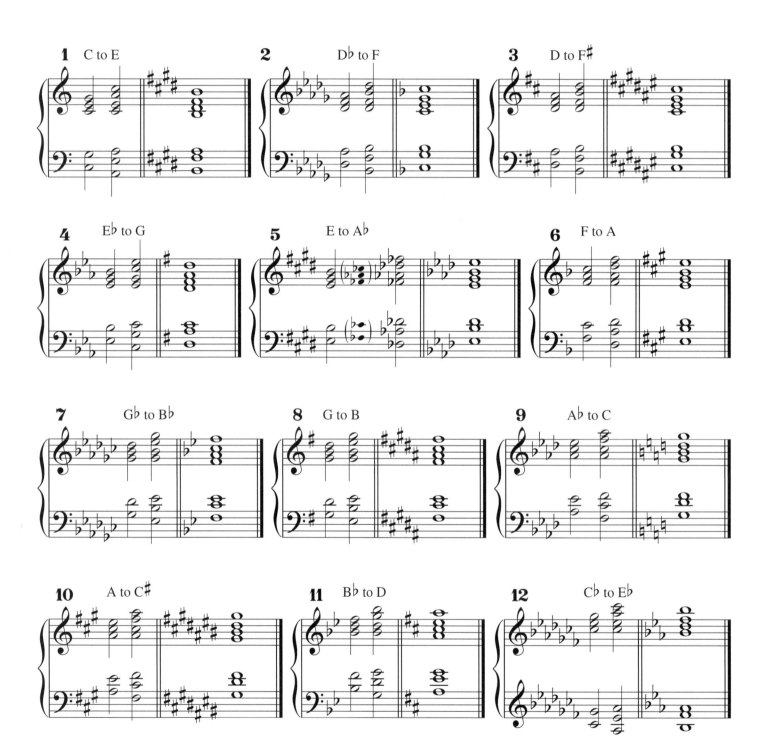

To modulate a major third up from minor keys:
1. Tonic triad (root position) of minor key of departure
2. Minor triad (root position) a minor third lower
3. Dominant seventh (root position) of new key

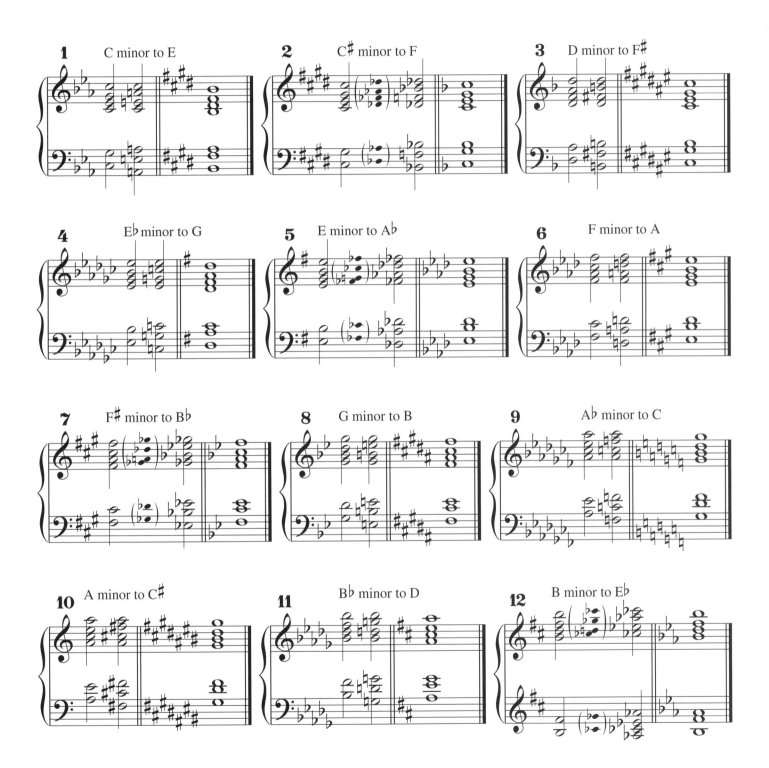

To modulate a major third down from major keys:
1. Tonic triad (root position) of major key of departure
2. Tonic triad of parallel minor (root position)
3. Dominant seventh (root position) of new key

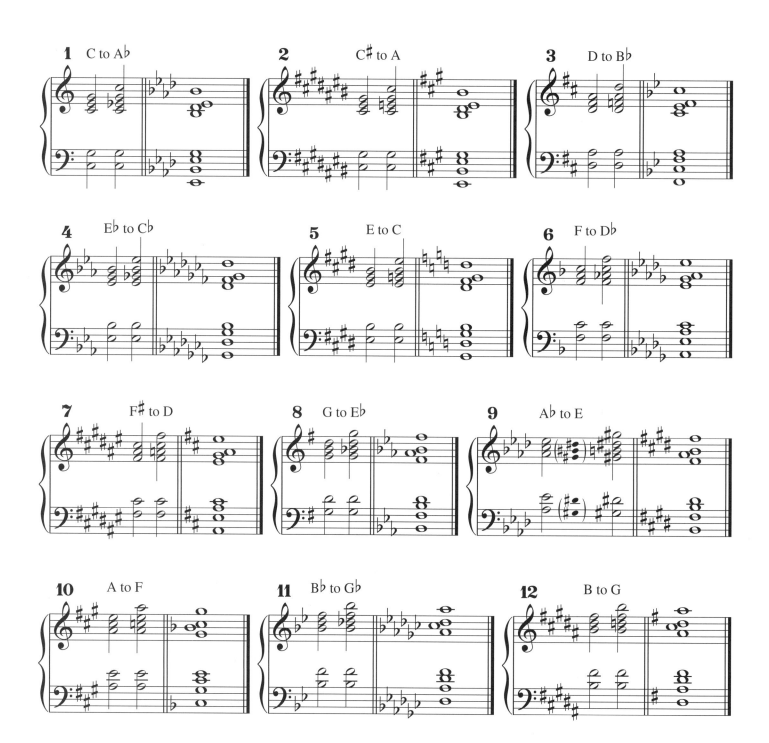

To modulate a major third down from minor keys:
1. Tonic triad (root position) of minor key of departure
2. Dominant seventh (root position) of new key

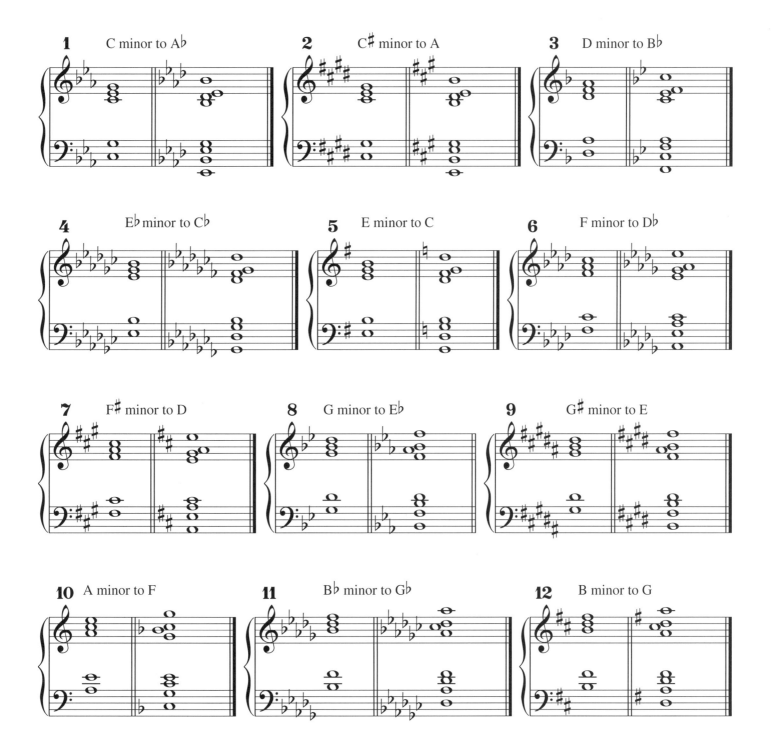

To modulate a perfect fourth up from major keys:
1. Tonic triad (root position) of major key of departure
2. Dominant seventh (root position) of new key

To modulate a perfect fourth up from minor keys:
1. Tonic triad (root position) of minor key of departure
2. Dominant seventh (root position) of new key

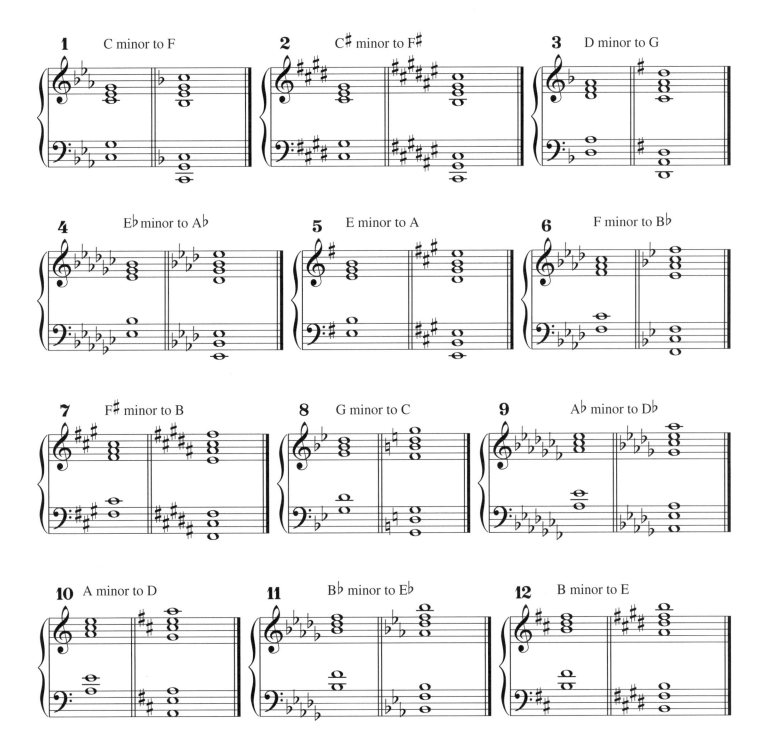

To modulate a perfect fourth down from major keys:
1. Tonic triad (root position) of major key of departure
2. Minor triad (root position) a minor third lower (relative minor)
3. Dominant seventh (root position) of new key

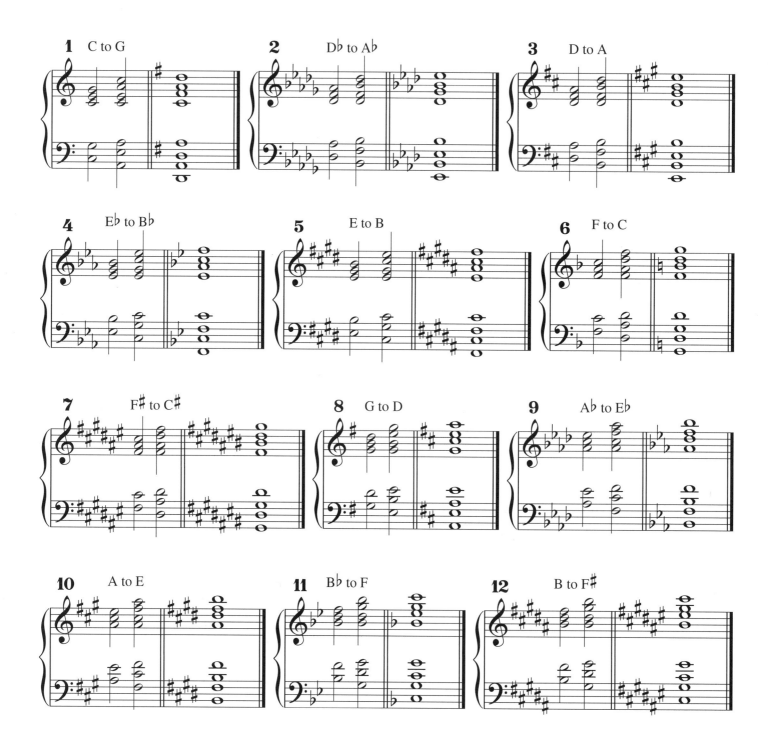

To modulate a perfect fourth down from minor keys:

1. Tonic triad (root position) of minor key of departure
2. Major triad (root position) a major third lower
3. Dominant seventh (root position) of new key

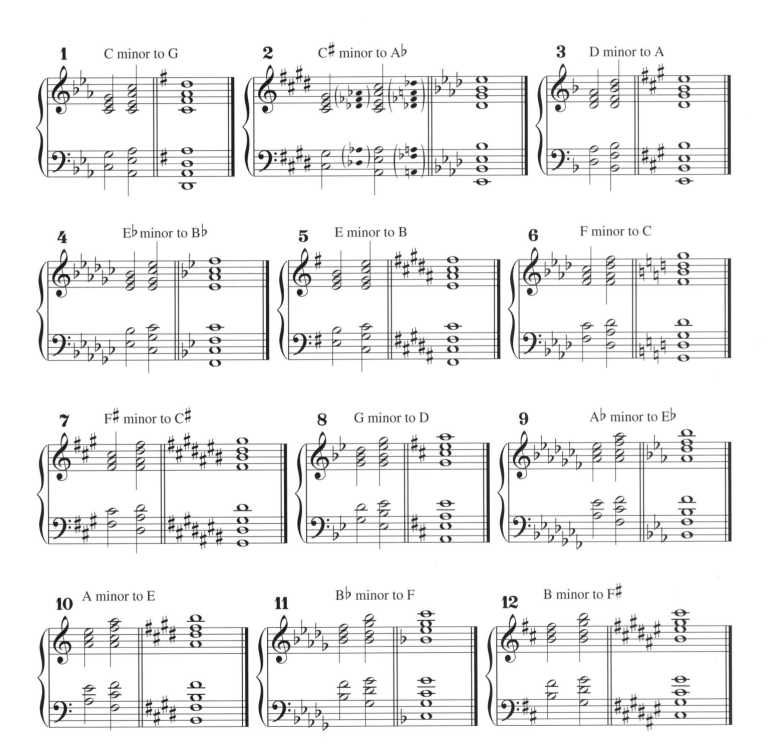

To modulate a diminished fifth (or augmented fourth) from major keys:
1. Tonic triad (root position) of major key of departure
2. Major triad (root position) on subdominant
3. Dominant seventh (root position) of new key

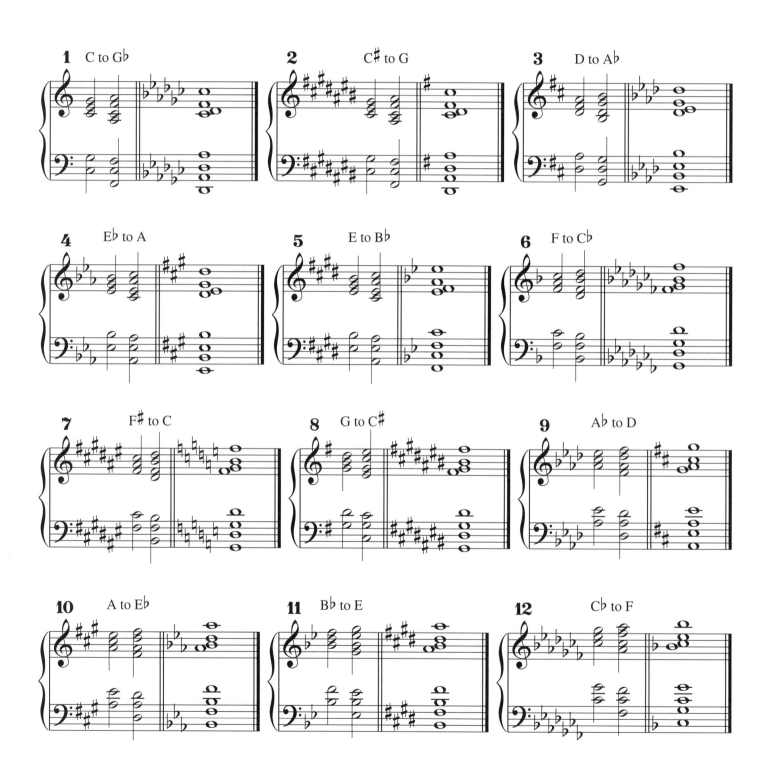

To modulate a diminished fifth (or augmented fourth) from minor keys:
1. Tonic triad (root position) of minor key of departure
2. Minor triad (root position) on subdominant
3. Dominant seventh (root position) of new key

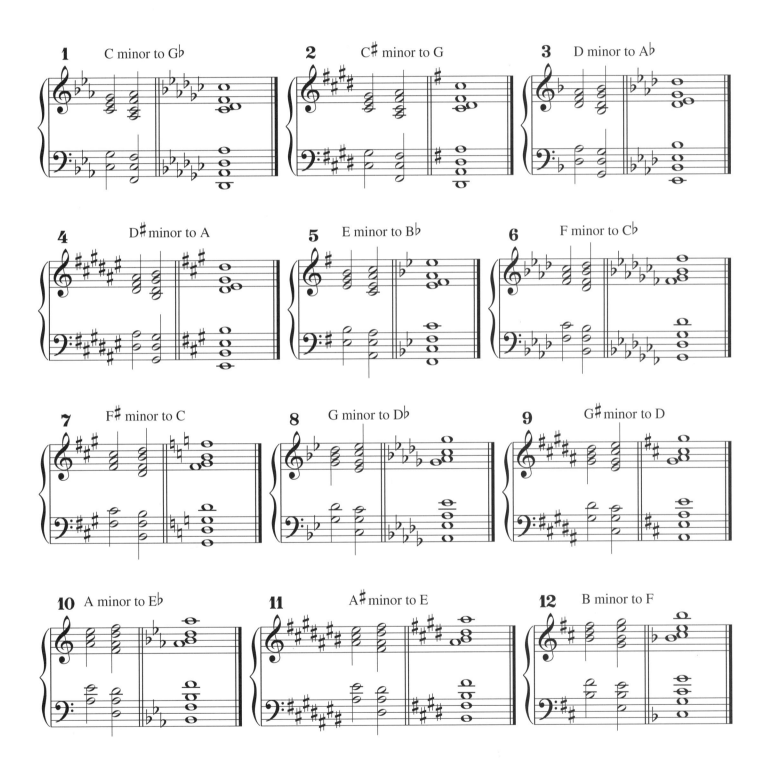

EXAMPLES OF MODULATION

The following examples suggest types of chords, arpeggios, broken figures, and other designs. It is of primary importance to emphasize the fact that all these examples can be used in every modulating formula.

In experimenting with the modulating process, one should bear in mind that the art of modulating implies the art of improvising; successful modulation, therefore, will depend on the skill and imagination of the player.

Modulating Instinct

If the instrumentalist is desirous to acquire a thorough understanding of the modulating process, he or she ought to try out each example in each modulating formula. As the instrumentalist goes along, he or she will come across melodic problems. For instance, in some cases, he or she will have to decide whether part of the modulating example would gain or lose by being transposed an octave higher or lower. Also, the instrumentalist will have to figure out how to attenuate abruptness, which generally is caused by bad voice leading or unjudicious use of common tones. To that effect, some of the right-hand chords—or arpeggios—might gain by being played in one of their inverted positions; this adjustment will open the way to a correct and successful use of common tones. By doing so, the instrumentalist will not only smooth out the modulation but will adorn it with a richer melodic sense. At times, a passing note will bring surprisingly good results. This is where musical instinct will be put to the test!

One might object that a treatise on the art of modulating ought to solve those problems and present them all written out, ready for use. Inasmuch as the amount of modulations goes far beyond theoretic conceptions, such an additional amount of work would have brought the size of this treatise to gigantic proportions without solving all possible problems. At all events, it is unquestionably more beneficial for the instrumentalist to unravel those problems on their own. Among other advantages, it will develop musical instinct and thorough understanding of an instrument.

EXAMPLE OF MODULATION A MINOR SECOND UP

E major to F

1. Tonic triad (root position) of major key of the composition just ended
2. Tonic triad of parallel minor (root position)
3. Dominant seventh (root position) of the key of the next composition

Arpeggio-type to be used in every modulating formula

Same arpeggio-type spread out

EXAMPLE OF MODULATION A MINOR SECOND DOWN

C minor to B

1. Tonic triad (root position) of minor key of the composition just ended
2. Minor triad (root position) a major third higher
3. Dominant seventh (root position) of the key of the next composition

Chord-type to be used in every modulating formula

EXAMPLE OF MODULATION A MAJOR SECOND UP

D minor to E

1. Tonic triad (root position) of minor key of the composition just ended
2. Minor triad (root position) a major third higher
3. Dominant seventh (root position) of the key of the next composition

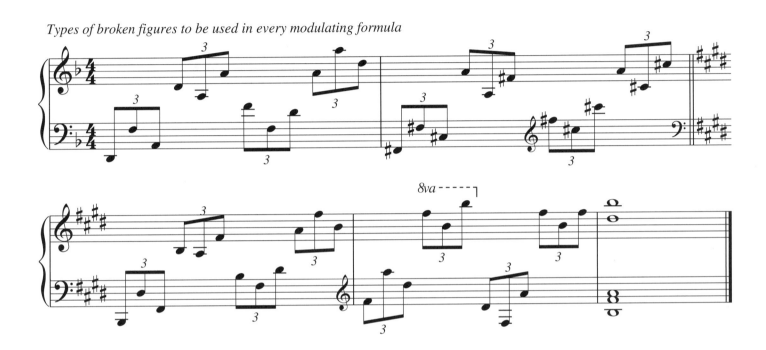

EXAMPLE OF MODULATION A MAJOR SECOND DOWN

D major to C

1. Tonic triad (root position) of major key of the composition just ended
2. Tonic triad of parallel minor (root position)
3. Dominant seventh (root position) of the key of the next composition

Barcarolle from "The Tales of Hoffmann"

EXAMPLE OF MODULATION A MINOR THIRD UP

D major to F

1. Tonic triad (root position) of major key of the composition just ended
2. Minor triad (root position) on subdominant
3. Dominant seventh (root position) of the key of the next composition

EXAMPLE OF MODULATION A MINOR THIRD DOWN

D major to B

1. Tonic triad (root position) of major key of the composition just ended
2. Minor triad (root position) one whole tone higher
3. Dominant seventh (root position) of the key of the next composition

MEMORANDUM

Thematic material for a modulation may be borrowed from the composition just played, but under no circumstances should it be borrowed from the forthcoming composition.

EXAMPLE OF MODULATION A PERFECT FOURTH UP

A minor to D
1. Tonic triad (root position) of minor key of the composition just ended
2. Dominant seventh (root position) of the key of the next composition

EXAMPLE OF MODULATION A PERFECT FOURTH DOWN

A minor to E
1. Tonic triad (root position) of minor key of the composition just ended
2. Major triad (root position) a major third lower
3. Dominant seventh (root position) of the key of the next composition

TYPES OF ARPEGGIOS FOR EXTENSION

To be used in every key.

TEN EXTENSIONS OF 10 SECONDS EACH AND A CODA

(in the rhythm of a Barcarolle)

To be used in every key, in part or in its entirety.

MODULATING ARPEGGIOS AND CHORDS

To be used in other keys.

TWO CADENZAS

To be used in other keys.

TEN FRAGMENTS OF DANCES AND FIVE EASY CHARACTER PIECES FOR KEYBOARD

Their Object

These fifteen pieces have been composed to fulfill a specific goal in relation to radio and television requirements: The goal concerns *timing*. These pieces can be *lengthened* by repeating a portion of the piece, or *shortened* by only playing part of it. Judicious repeats or cuts will depend on the player's good taste and musical instinct.

Waltz Accompaniment

Petite Valse

Gavotte

Menuet

Polka

Siciliana

Bolero

Seguidilla

Tango

Rumba

Lullaby
(Berceuse)

Rêverie
(in remembrance of Gabriel Fauré)

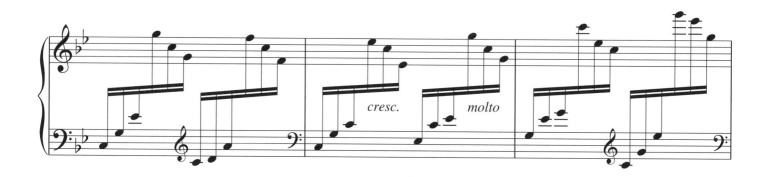

Carillon

Grandmother's Spinning Wheel

Florentine Music Box

PLAY PIANO LIKE A PRO!

AMAZING PHRASING – KEYBOARD
50 Ways to Improve Your Improvisational Skills
by Debbie Denke
Amazing Phrasing is for any keyboard player interested in learning how to improvise and how to improve their creative phrasing. This method is divided into three parts: melody, harmony, and rhythm & style. The companion CD contains 44 full-band demos for listening, as well as many play-along examples so you can practice improvising over various musical styles and progressions.
00842030 Book/CD Pack $16.95

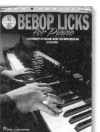

BEBOP LICKS FOR PIANO
A Dictionary of Melodic Ideas for Improvisation
by Les Wise
Written for the musician who is interested in acquiring a firm foundation for playing jazz, this unique book/CD pack presents over 800 licks. By building up a vocabulary of these licks, players can connect them together in endless possibilities to form larger phrases and complete solos. The book includes piano notation, and the CD contains helpful note-for-note demos of every lick.
00311854 Book/CD Pack $16.99

BOOGIE WOOGIE FOR BEGINNERS
by Frank Paparelli
A short easy method for learning to play boogie woogie, designed for the beginner and average pianist. Includes: exercises for developing left-hand bass • 25 popular boogie woogie bass patterns • arrangements of "Down the Road a Piece" and "Answer to the Prayer" by well-known pianists • a glossary of musical terms for dynamics, tempo and style.
00120517 .... $7.95

INTROS, ENDINGS & TURNAROUNDS FOR KEYBOARD
Essential Phrases for Swing, Latin, Jazz Waltz, and Blues Styles
by John Valerio
Learn the intros, endings and turnarounds that all of the pros know and use! This new keyboard instruction book by John Valerio covers swing styles, ballads, Latin tunes, jazz waltzes, blues, major and minor keys, vamps and pedal tones, and more.
00290525 .... $12.95

JAZZ PIANO VOICINGS
An Essential Resource for Aspiring Jazz Musicians
by Rob Mullins
The jazz idiom can often appear mysterious and difficult for musicians who were trained to play other types of music. Long-time performer and educator Rob Mullins helps players enter the jazz world by providing voicings that will help the player develop skills in the jazz genre and start sounding professional right away – without years of study! Includes a "Numeric Voicing Chart," chord indexes in all 12 keys, info about what range of the instrument you can play chords in, and a beginning approach to bass lines.
00310914 .... $19.95

101 KEYBOARD TIPS
Stuff All the Pros Know and Use
by Craig Weldon
Ready to take your keyboard playing to the next level? This book will show you how. *101 Keyboard Tips* presents valuable how-to insight that players of all styles and levels can benefit from. The text, photos, music, diagrams and accompanying CD provide an essential, easy-to-use resource for a variety of topics, including: techniques, improvising and soloing, equipment, practicing, ear training, performance, theory, and much more.
00310933 Book/CD Pack $14.95

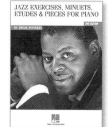

OSCAR PETERSON – JAZZ EXERCISES, MINUETS, ETUDES & PIECES FOR PIANO
Legendary jazz pianist Oscar Peterson has long been devoted to the education of piano students. In this book he offers dozens of pieces designed to empower the student, whether novice or classically trained, with the technique needed to become an accomplished jazz pianist.
00311225 .... $12.99

PIANO AEROBICS
by Wayne Hawkins
Piano Aerobics is a set of exercises that introduces students to many popular styles of music, including jazz, salsa, swing, rock, blues, new age, gospel, stride, and bossa nova. In addition, there is a CD with accompaniment tracks featuring professional musicians playing in those styles.
00311863 Book/CD Pack $19.99

PIANO FITNESS
A Complete Workout
by Mark Harrison
This book will give you a thorough technical workout, while having fun at the same time! The accompanying CD allows you to play along with a rhythm section as you practice your scales, arpeggios, and chords in all keys. Instead of avoiding technique exercises because they seem too tedious or difficult, you'll look forward to playing them. Various voicings and rhythmic settings, which are extremely useful in a variety of pop and jazz styles, are also introduced.
00311995 Book/CD Pack $19.99

THE TOTAL KEYBOARD PLAYER
A Complete Guide to the Sounds, Styles & Sonic Spectrum
by Dave Adler
Do you play the keyboards in your sleep? Do you live for the feel of the keys beneath your fingers? If you answered in the affirmative, then read on, brave musical warrior! All you seek is here: the history, the tricks, the stops, the patches, the plays, the holds, the fingering, the dynamics, the exercises, the magic. Everything you always wanted to know about keyboards, all in one amazing key-centric compendium.
00311977 Book/CD Pack $19.99

HAL•LEONARD®
7777 W. BLUEMOUND RD. P.O. BOX 13819
MILWAUKEE, WISCONSIN 53213

Prices, contents, and availability subject to change without notice.

www.halleonard.com

jazz piano solos series

INCLUDES CHORD NAMES! Each volume features exciting new arrangements of the songs which helped define a style.

vol. 1 miles davis — second edition
New piano solo arrangements of 19 classic tunes by the great Miles Davis: All Blues • Blue in Green • Boplicity (Be Bop Lives) • Circle • Dig • Eighty One • Four • Freddie Freeloader • Half Nelson • Miles • Milestones • Nardis • So What • Solar • Somethin' Else • Tune Up • and more.
00306521 Piano Solo.........$15.99

vol. 2 jazz blues — second edition
This collection presents 26 jazz-blues classics served up for solo piano. Songs: All Blues • Au Privave • Birk's Works • Blue Monk • Blues in the Closet • C-Jam Blues • Freddie Freeloader • Mr. P.C. • Now's the Time • Straight No Chaser • and more.
00306522 Piano Solo.........$15.99

vol. 3 latin jazz
17 Latin jazz classics, including: Brazil (Xavier Cugat, Django Reinhardt) • Manteca (Dizzy Gillespie, Cal Tjader) • Mas Que Nada (Dizzy Gillespie) • Perfidia (Perez Prado, Nat King Cole) • Triste (Antonio Carlos Jobim, Cal Tjader) • and more.
00310621 Piano Solo.........$15.99

vol. 4 bebop jazz
25 classics from jazz masters of the '40s and '50s, such as Charlie Parker, Dizzy Gillespie, Thelonious Monk, Sonny Rollins, Ella Fitzgerald and others. Tunes include: Anthropology • Au Privave • Billie's Bounce • Doxy • Half Nelson • In Walked Bud • Lady Bird • Lemon Drop • Well You Needn't • Woodyn' You • and more.
00310709 Piano Solo.........$15.99

vol. 5 cool jazz — second edition
23 tunes from the '50s and '60s jazz cats who invented "cool," including: All Blues (Miles Davis, George Benson) • A Ballad (Gerry Mulligan, Stan Getz) • Con Alma (Dizzy Gillespie, Stan Getz) • Epistrophy (Thelonious Monk) • Nardis (Bill Evans, Joe Henderson) • Take Five (Dave Brubeck, George Benson) • and more.
00310710 Piano Solo.........$15.99

vol. 6 hard bop
18 jazz classics from the '50s and '60s, including: The Champ (Dizzy Gillespie, Jimmy Smith) • Giant Steps (John Coltrane, Tommy Flanagan) • Mercy, Mercy, Mercy (Cannonball Adderley, Joe Zawinul) • Song for My Father (Kenny Burrell, Horace Silver) • This Here (Bobby Timmons, Cannonball Adderly) • and more.
00310711 Piano Solo.........$15.99

vol. 7 smooth jazz
19 contemporary favorites: Cast Your Fate to the Wind (David Benoit) • Just the Two of Us (Grover Washington, Jr.) • Morning Dance (Spyro Gyra) • Mountain Dance (Dave Grusin) • This Masquerade (George Benson) • We're in This Love Together (Al Jarreau) • and more.
00310727 Piano Solo.........$15.99

vol. 8 jazz pop
New jazz piano arrangements of 22 classic pop songs, including: Blackbird • Don't Know Why • Fields of Gold • Isn't She Lovely • It's Too Late • New York State of Mind • On Broadway • Oye Como Va • Roxanne • What a Fool Believes • You Are So Beautiful • and more.
00311786 Piano Solo.........$15.99

vol. 9 duke ellington
New piano solo arrangements of 24 beloved Duke Ellington songs, including: Caravan • Don't Get Around Much Anymore • It Don't Mean a Thing • Mood Indigo • Satin Doll • Take the "A" Train • and more.
00311787 Piano Solo.........$15.99

vol. 10 jazz ballads
Fresh solo piano arrangements of 24 favorite ballads in a jazz style, including: Body and Soul • I Guess I'll Hang My Tears Out to Dry • Misty • My Funny Valentine • The Nearness of You • When I Fall in Love • and more.
00311788 Piano Solo.........$15.99

vol. 11 soul jazz
22 tunes full of soul, including: Chitlins Con Carne • Dat Dere • Five Spot After Dark • The "In" Crowd • The Midnight Special • Sister Sadie • Soultrane • Unchain My Heart • What'd I Say • You Are My Sunshine • and more.
00311789 Piano Solo.........$15.99

vol. 12 swinging jazz
Hip new piano solo arrangements of 24 swinging classics, including: Ain't That a Kick in the Head • All of Me • Beyond the Sea • Bluesette • Come Fly with Me • It's Only a Paper Moon • Just in Time • Route 66 • Steppin' Out with My Baby • Witchcraft • and more.
00311797 Piano Solo.........$15.99

vol. 13 jazz gems
21 jazz classics arranged for solo piano with chord names: All Too Soon • Confirmation • Don't Explain • Line for Lyons • Little Sunflower • Naima (Niema) • A Night in Tunisia • Nuages • Spain • Stablemates • Stolen Moments • Topsy • Two Bass Hit • and more.
00311899 Piano Solo.........$15.99

vol. 14 jazz classics
Rich piano solo arrangements with chord names of 21 of the best jazz gems of all time: Bernie's Tune • Birdland • Donna Lee • Footprints • Impressions • On Green Dolphin Street • Red Clay • Robbin's Nest • St. Thomas • Turn Out the Stars • Yardbird Suite • and more.
00311900 Piano Solo.........$15.99

vol. 15 bossa nova
Solo arrangements with chord names of 20 swinging Latin standards: Agua De Beber • Call Me • Estate • The Girl from Ipanema • Meditation • Quiet Nights of Quiet Stars • Watch What Happens • Wave • more!
00311906 Piano Solo.........$15.99

vol. 16 disney
Cool jazzy solo arrangements with chord names for 22 Disney favorites, including: Alice in Wonderland • The Bare Necessities • Beauty and the Beast • Chim Chim Cher-ee • Some Day My Prince Will Come • When You Wish upon a Star • and more.
00312121 Piano Solo.........$16.99

vol. 17 antonio carlos jobim
20 Jobim favorites, including: Água De Beber (Water to Drink) • Águas De Março (Waters of March) • Bim-Bom • The Girl from Ipanema (Garôta De Ipanema) • How Insensitive (Insensatez) • Meditation (Meditacao) • Slightly Out of Tune (Desafinado) • more.
00312122 Piano Solo.........$15.99

vol. 18 modern jazz quartet
20 MJQ favorites arranged for piano solo, including: Afternoon in Paris • Bags' Groove • Bluesology • Concorde • Connie's Blues • Django • Echoes • La Ronde • Milano • The Queen's Fancy • Reunion Blues • Skating in Central Park • Vendome • and more.
00307270 Piano Solo.........$16.99

vol. 19 bill evans
24 essential Evans standards arranged for piano solo, including: Autumn Leaves • But Beautiful • Here's That Rainy Day • In a Sentimental Mood • My Foolish Heart • Night and Day • Suicide Is Painless (Song from M*A*S*H) • Witchcraft • and more.
00307273 Piano Solo.........$16.99

vol. 20 gypsy jazz
Over 20 swinging Gypsy favorites, including: After You've Gone • Ain't Misbehavin' • Are You in the Mood • Crepuscule • Daphne • Django's Tiger • Djangology • Honeysuckle Rose • Minor Swing • Nuages • Swing de Paris • Swing Guitar • Ultrafox • and more.
00307289 Piano Solo.........$16.99

vol. 22 classic jazz
Lush piano solo arrangements with chord names for 23 spectacular jazz gems: Bouncing with Bud • Dolphin Dance • Filthy McNasty • Lady Day • Minor Swing • Rifftide • Un Poco Loco • Up Jumped Spring • Valse Hot • Watermelon Man • and many more!
00001529 Piano Solo.........$16.99

vol. 25 christmas songs
21 holiday classics arranged for jazz piano: Blue Christmas • Christmas Time Is Here • Have Yourself a Merry Little Christmas • I'll Be Home for Christmas • My Favorite Things • Santa Baby • Silver Bells • White Christmas • and more.
00101790 Piano Solo.........$16.99

HAL•LEONARD CORPORATION
7777 W. BLUEMOUND RD. P.O. BOX 13819 MILWAUKEE, WI 53213

Prices, contents and availability subject to change without notice.

www.halleonard.com

0612

KEYBOARD STYLE SERIES

THE COMPLETE GUIDE WITH CD!

These book/CD packs provide focused lessons that contain valuable how-to insight, essential playing tips, and beneficial information for all players. From comping to soloing, comprehensive treatment is given to each subject. The companion CD features many of the examples in the book performed either solo or with a full band.

BEBOP JAZZ PIANO
by John Valerio

This book provides detailed information for bebop and jazz keyboardists on: chords and voicings, harmony and chord progressions, scales and tonality, common melodic figures and patterns, comping, characteristic tunes, the styles of Bud Powell and Thelonious Monk, and more. Includes 5 combo performances at the end of the book.
00290535 Book/CD Pack....................................$18.95

BEGINNING ROCK KEYBOARD
by Mark Harrison

This comprehensive book/CD package will teach you the basic skills needed to play beginning rock keyboard. From comping to soloing, you'll learn the theory, the tools, and the techniques used by the pros. The accompanying CD demonstrates most of the music examples in the book.
00311922 Book/CD Pack....................................$14.99

BLUES PIANO
by Mark Harrison

With this book/CD pack, you'll learn the theory, the tools, and even the tricks that the pros use to play the blues. You also get seven complete tunes to jam with on the CD. Covers: scales and chords; left-hand patterns; walking bass; endings and turnarounds; right-hand techniques; how to solo with blues scales; crossover licks; and more.
00311007 Book/CD Pack....................................$17.95

BRAZILIAN PIANO
by Robert Willey and Alfredo Cardim

Brazilian Piano teaches elements of some of the most appealing Brazilian musical styles: choro, samba, and bossa nova. It starts with rhythmic training to develop the fundamental groove of Brazilian music. Next, examples build up a rhythmic and harmonic vocabulary that can be used when playing the original songs that follow.
00311469 Book/CD Pack....................................$19.99

CONTEMPORARY JAZZ PIANO
by Mark Harrison

From comping to soloing, you'll learn the theory, the tools, and the techniques used by the pros. The full band tracks on the CD feature the rhythm section on the left channel and the piano on the right channel, so that you can play along with the band.
00311848 Book/CD Pack....................................$17.99

COUNTRY PIANO
by Mark Harrison

Learn the theory, the tools, and the tricks used by the pros to get that authentic country sound. This book/CD pack covers: scales and chords, walkup and walkdown patterns, comping in traditional and modern country, Nashville "fretted piano" techniques and more. At the end, you'll get to jam along with seven complete tunes.
00311052 Book/CD Pack....................................$17.95

GOSPEL PIANO
by Kurt Cowling

This comprehensive book/CD pack provides you with the tools you need to play in a variety of authentic gospel styles, through a study of rhythmic devices, grooves, melodic and harmonic techniques, and formal design. The accompanying CD features over 90 tracks, including piano examples as well as the full gospel band.
00311327 Book/CD Pack....................................$17.95

INTRO TO JAZZ PIANO
by Mark Harrison

This comprehensive book/CD is the perfect *Intro to Jazz Piano*. From comping to soloing, you'll learn the theory, the tools, and the techniques used by the pros. The accompanying CD demonstrates most of the music examples in the book. The full band tracks feature the rhythm section on the left channel and the piano on the right channel, so that you can play along with the band.
00312088 Book/CD Pack....................................$16.99

JAZZ-BLUES PIANO
by Mark Harrison

This comprehensive book will teach you the basic skills needed to play jazz-blues piano. Topics covered include: scales and chords • harmony and voicings • progressions and comping • melodies and soloing • characteristic stylings.
00311243 Book/CD Pack....................................$17.95

JAZZ-ROCK KEYBOARD
by T. Lavitz

Learn what goes into mixing the power and drive of rock music with the artistic elements of jazz improvisation in this comprehensive book and CD package. This instructional tool delves into scales and modes, and how they can be used with various chord progressions to develop the best in soloing chops.
00290536 Book/CD Pack....................................$17.95

LATIN JAZZ PIANO
by John Valerio

This book is divided into three sections. The first covers Afro-Cuban (Afro-Caribbean) jazz, the second section deals with Brazilian influenced jazz – Bossa Nova and Samba, and the third contains lead sheets of the tunes and instructions for the play-along CD.
00311345 Book/CD Pack....................................$17.99

POST-BOP JAZZ PIANO
by John Valerio

This book/CD pack will teach you the basic skills needed to play post-bop jazz piano. Learn the theory, the tools, and the tricks used by the pros to play in the style of Bill Evans, Thelonious Monk, Herbie Hancock, McCoy Tyner, Chick Corea and others. Topics covered include: chord voicings, scales and tonality, modality, and more.
00311005 Book/CD Pack....................................$17.95

PROGRESSIVE ROCK KEYBOARD
by Dan Maske

From the classic sounds of the '70s to modern progressive stylings, this book/CD provides you with the theory and technique to play and compose in a multitude of prog rock styles. You'll learn how soloing techniques, form, rhythmic and metrical devices, harmony, and counterpoint all come together to make this style of rock the unique and exciting genre it is.
00311307 Book/CD Pack....................................$17.95

Prices, contents, and availability subject to change without notice.

Visit Hal Leonard online at
www.halleonard.com

FOR MORE INFORMATION, SEE YOUR LOCAL MUSIC DEALER, OR WRITE TO:

HAL•LEONARD CORPORATION
7777 W. BLUEMOUND RD. P.O. BOX 13819 MILWAUKEE, WI 53213

R&B KEYBOARD
by Mark Harrison

From soul to funk to disco to pop, you'll learn the theory, the tools, and the tricks used by the pros with this book/CD pack. Topics covered include: scales and chords, harmony and voicings, progressions and comping, rhythmic concepts, characteristic stylings, the development of R&B, and more! Includes seven songs.
00310881 Book/CD Pack....................................$17.95

ROCK KEYBOARD
by Scott Miller

Learn to comp or solo in any of your favorite rock styles. Listen to the CD to hear your parts fit in with the total groove of the band. Includes 99 tracks! Covers: classic rock, pop/rock, blues rock, Southern rock, hard rock, progressive rock, alternative rock and heavy metal.
00310823 Book/CD Pack....................................$17.95

ROCK 'N' ROLL PIANO
by Andy Vinter

Take your place alongside Fats Domino, Jerry Lee Lewis, Little Richard, and other legendary players of the '50s and '60s! This book/CD pack covers: left-hand patterns; basic rock 'n' roll progressions; right-hand techniques; straight eighths vs. swing eighths; glisses, crushed notes, rolls, note clusters and more. Includes six complete tunes.
00310912 Book/CD Pack....................................$17.95

SALSA PIANO
by Hector Martignon

From traditional Cuban music to the more modern Puerto Rican and New York styles, you'll learn the all-important rhythmic patterns of salsa and how to apply them to the piano. The book provides historical, geographical and cultural background info, and the 50+-track CD includes piano examples and a full salsa band percussion section.
00311049 Book/CD Pack....................................$17.95

SMOOTH JAZZ PIANO
by Mark Harrison

Learn the skills you need to play smooth jazz piano – the theory, the tools, and the tricks used by the pros. Topics covered include: scales and chords; harmony and voicings; progressions and comping; rhythmic concepts; melodies and soloing; characteristic stylings; discussions on jazz evolution.
00311095 Book/CD Pack....................................$17.95

STRIDE & SWING PIANO
by John Valerio

Learn the styles of the stride and swing piano masters, such as Scott Joplin, Jimmy Yancey, Pete Johnson, Jelly Roll Morton, James P. Johnson, Fats Waller, Teddy Wilson, and Art Tatum. This book/CD pack covers classic ragtime, early blues and boogie woogie, New Orleans jazz and more. Includes 14 songs.
00310882 Book/CD Pack....................................$17.95